DISCARD

W9-CTS-945

what you will learn from this book

Do you know that two basketballs will almost go through a basketball hoop at the same time? Well, it is true. That doesn't mean, though, that it's easy to shoot one ball through the basket.

It's even harder when you're short and the basket's 10 feet off the ground. Your hands are also smaller than they will be when you are bigger, stronger, and better coordinated a few years from now.

Can you still learn to shoot a basketball properly now? Sure, if you follow some suggestions and admit you can't correctly shoot the same shot your 18-year-old brother or neighbor puts up.

1

theset shot

text/Paul J. Deegan
illustrations/
Harold Henriksen

Consultant: Lloyd Raymond, B.A., Augsburg College; M.S., Physical Education, Mankato State College; Instructor in Physical Education and Head Basketball Coach, Mankato State College.

CREATIVE EDUCATION
Mankato, Minnesota

THIS BOOK
PROPERTY OF
HACIENDA SCHOOL

Published by Creative Educational Society, Inc., 123 South Broad Street,
Mankato, Minnesota 56001. Copyright © 1975 by Creative Educational Society,
Inc. International copyrights reserved in all countries. No part of this book may be
reproduced in any form without written permission from the publisher. Printed in
the United States. Distributed by Childrens Press, 1224 West Van Buren Street,
Chicago, Illinois 60607.

Library of Congress 75-11913   ISBN: O-87191-433-6
Library of Congress Cataloging in Publication Data
Deegan, Paul J   1937-
    The set shot.
    SUMMARY: Gives instructions in the techniques of shooting a basket.
    1. Basketball—Juvenile literature. (1. Basketball) I. Henriksen, Harold. II. Title.
GV885.1.D425   796.32'3   75-11913   ISBN O-87191-433-6

For Lisa, Mike, and John – may participation in athletics bring
you as much enjoyment as it has brought your dad.

Throwing a ball at a basket is natural. Shooting a basketball is not. The fundamentals must be learned, then practiced until they become instinctive. You will be able to put the ball in the basket sometimes even if your technique is bad. But if you want to be good, you'll need to master the fundamentals.

The one-handed set shot or push shot is the fundamental shot in learning how to shoot. However, you can watch many high school, college, and professional basketball games today without ever seeing a set shot, except at the free-throw line. This is because today most players shoot only jump shots. The reason is that the jump shot is quicker to get off.

Yet the fundamentals involved in the set shot are basic to the jump shot, the lay-up, and the free throw, the other important shots in a basketball game. Former pro superstar Jerry West has called the set shot "the most basic shot."

Young boys and girls can master the set shot if they do two things: use a junior basketball and shoot at a shorter basket. The young player who is serious about becoming a good shooter will try to do this if it's possible. We'll say more about this later.

body must
be under
control

Shooting appears to be almost entirely an arm and hand action. The legs, though, are essential. A shooter must have good body balance; his body must be under control. The good shooter shoots the ball the same each time. The exception, especially noticeable when watching pro players, occurs when the shooter is under extreme pressure. Remember, though, that the Walt Fraziers and Julius Ervings have such great physical ability that they can control their body in situations where the average player cannot.

If you're going to shoot the same way each time, you can't worry about being off balance. So the number one step in shooting is to bring your body under control. Your body must be relaxed, yet in balance.

You accomplish this by taking the proper stance. Your feet should be shoulder-width apart. The right foot (for a right-handed shooter) is slightly ahead of the left. The left foot is turned out slightly. Your head must remain at mid-point between your feet all during the shot. If you let your head move off to one side or the other, you will throw your body off balance.

The power for your shot is provided through your legs. The power is controlled by flexing your knees. The knees should be slightly flexed or bent as you get ready for your set shot. Lean forward slightly, but don't tilt forward. Your weight must be up on the balls of your feet.

You grip the ball in your fingertips. The hand is behind and down on the ball; the fingers don't come over the top of it. The hand is more to the right side of the ball if you're right-handed. The thumb and the index finger (the finger next to the thumb) form a V.

The ball should never touch the palm of your shooting hand. You should be able to look at the ball in your hand and see a space between the fingers and the palm. You must shoot the ball off your fingertips, not push it off the palm of your hand. The fingertips give you control and "touch" on the ball. The thumb of the shooting hand is just under the ball. The wrist is relaxed.

Your other hand serves as a balancing machine. Held underneath the ball on the left side (for a right-hander) of the ball, it

fingertips grip ball

protects the ball from a defender. The non-shooting hand remains in contact with the ball until the moment before you release it.

Keep the elbow of your shooting arm in front of you and on a line with the basket as you prepare to shoot. It should be close to, but not touching, your body. The biggest mistake young players often make is to cock their elbow out to the side. They do this hoping to get more power, forgetting that the power should come from bending the knees. If you push your elbow out to the side, you lose control and direction of the shot.

The position of the elbow in shooting is perhaps the easiest way to determine whether or not a player is using the proper shooting technique.

Bring the ball out in front of the body to a position between the shoulder and the eye on your shooting side. Hold the ball at just about eye level. This is the place from which you want to release the ball.

watch elbow position

     One thing shooters must realize is that the inside of the hoop (18 inches) is almost twice as large as the diameter of the basketball (about 9½ inches). Therefore there is really quite a bit of room for error on a shot. The ball doesn't have to fall into the exact middle of the basket to go through it. You can be off many inches and still score.

13

When you're going to shoot, your goal is to put the ball in the basket. A very important part of shooting, something young players may forget, is concentration on the basket. You must lock your eyes on the basket and keep them there until the shot is made or begins bouncing off.

Where do you direct your eyes on the basket? Coaches and shooters disagree about the best spot to aim at. Many say just over the front rim. Others say shoot for the middle of the basket, called the hole. Some say the back rim. Just over the front rim or the hole are probably your best bet. If you aim for just over the front rim and overshoot a little, the ball will still fall easily through the hoop. However, this is something you're going to have to decide for yourself. Do whatever works best for you.

As you bring the ball to the position from which you want to release it, you bend your knees more. As you release the ball, you straighten your knees and go up on the balls of your feet, providing the power for the shot. If your feet leave the floor, that's okay. But spring off your feet, don't jump. The further away you are from the basket, obviously the more power your legs will have to provide. This will often cause you to finish your shot with your feet in the air. You will be able to tell how much leg action you need when you shoot from different places on the floor.

You do not want to provide power by swinging your elbow out or pushing the ball further in front of you. Your goal should be to have the very same arm motion every time you shoot, no matter where you're standing. If you're close to the basket, you won't need much leg action. If you're further out, you'll need quite a bit.

Just before you release the ball, you must cock your wrist which is kept back behind the elbow. The elbow is still in close to the body but slightly ahead of the wrist. The ball is still in front of you between shoulder and eyes and at eye level. This is the position from which you shoot. As you begin to release the ball, the wrist moves ahead of the elbow. Snap the wrist down. The wrist snap produces follow through.

shoot from
this
position

As you release the ball, you roll it off your fingertips. The ball should come off your fingertips in what is best described as a backward motion. This sounds difficult, but it is easy, almost natural to do. You flip the fingers at the moment of release. This action produces backspin on the ball.

Backspin along with the arc of the shot gives you "touch" — the soft, floating movement of the ball. You do not want to bang the ball up to the basket. If the shot is not perfect, the ball will fly off the rim. If the shot has touch, it will bounce softly off the rim and may times will fall back through the hoop.

The index finger, the one next to the thumb, will be the last finger off the ball. This finger gives the most control to your shot. Get in the habit of pointing this finger at the basket after you release the ball. This will increase your accuracy.

The shooter must also worry about getting the shot high enough. The basket is 10-feet high, and the ball must come down into it from an arc above it. Young players naturally put a pretty good arc on the ball because they are short. There is no perfect arc. What you want to do is avoid a flat shot. A flat shot requires great accuracy and will

come off hard if it doesn't go in the basket. Find the arc which works for you and try to keep it the same on each shot.

Jerry Lucas of the New York Knicks has a ridiculously high arc when he shoots from outside. It works for him, so it's fine. But it's not necessary. Jerry West, the former Los Angeles Laker great, often shot very flat. However, West had uncanny accuracy.

There are so many things for a beginning player to consider when he's learning to shoot. You might wonder how you can ever keep them straight in your mind.

You can't if you try to consider them all at the same time. You have to concentrate on a couple things at a time. Pick out one or two things and work on them for a day. Single out something else another day. Spend some time working on all the fundamentals. You will find that some things don't need much attention. They'll come pretty naturally. Concentrate on those that come harder for you.

After you repeat this process many times, the fundamentals will become habits. You will have begun to do them instinctively. You will still find yourself thinking about them often. That's fine. When you think about your elbow position, for instance, check it out. If you're doing it correctly, forget it.

Even professional players may go back to the fundamentals when they're having shooting problems.

One thing you'll always have to work at is concentration. If you're going to shoot, think about it; zero in on the basket. This is a must for successful shooting.

Although you will seldom see any-
thing but a jump shot in basketball games,
the best thing a young player can do is forget
about the jump shot. This may not make much
sense to you. Why not start right away on the
shot that everyone shoots?

The answer is that you don't have
sufficient strength or coordination to do it
properly. As a general rule you will be better
off to wait until the last part of your seventh
grade year before you start working on your
jump shot.

Spend your time instead working on
the set shot. If you can master this shot, it
will be easy to move into the jump shot later.

THIS BOOK
PROPERTY OF
HACIENDA SCHOOL

Using a junior basketball and a shorter basket really help a young player learn to shoot properly. The junior basketball looks about the same as a regulation ball, but it is slightly smaller. You will be able to control it in your hands much better.

Many school gyms have some baskets less than 10-feet high. Don't say those are only for "little kids." If you're in fourth, fifth, even sixth grade, you're still small compared to the six-foot, six-four, and six-ten high school, college, and pro players who shoot at a 10-foot basket. If your school gym doesn't have a shorter basket, suggest it to your gym teacher.

If your family is thinking about putting up a backboard and basket at your house, ask about an adjustable pole. You can start the basket lower and move it up as you grow older. One college coach strongly recommends a 9-foot-high basket even for 12-year-olds.

If you just want to fool around with a basketball, it probably won't make much difference if the ball's too big, the basket's too high, and you're not physically able to shoot a jump shot. But if you want to be a player, which means learning how to shoot properly, then these things will make a great deal of difference in the years ahead.

Free throw shooting will be difficult for the younger, smaller player if he has to shoot the 15-foot long shot at the regular 10-foot high basket. If you can use a shorter basket, you can probably start practicing free throws after you have learned to shoot successfully closer to the basket.

Free throws are important because they are just that — a free chance to score. Your goal should be to make 8 out of 10 free throws. A player who can make 5 of 10 field goals is considered a good shooter. Five of 10 free throws is not good.

A free throw can be shot anyway you want from any place behind the free throw line. Most players use a set shot and stand at the line directly in front of the basket. They use the set shot because it provides the best balance. They stand as close as they can and in line with the basket because this should be the easiest shot.

The most important thing in shooting free throws is concentration. You must learn

relax!
then
shoot!

through experience to block everything from your mind except the rim of the basket. Once you have mastered the fundamentals of the set shot, you shouldn't have to think about the shot itself. Lock your eyes on the basket, concentrate, and shoot with confidence.

Though you must concentrate, you must be relaxed. Often you're tired or have been fouled and knocked to the floor. Many players dribble the ball a few times to relax themselves. Some also take a deep breath. Find what works for you and do it.

Practice is a must for a player who wants to be a good free throw shooter. You must develop a groove or rhythm to your shot so you can shoot free throws with confidence. Practice shooting free throws when you're tired. You will often be tired when you get a free throw late in a game.

creative
education
sports
instructional
series for
young
people